SOULSPECTION

To:
KATO'S
Thank you for your
support ... Love & light!!
Soulfully yours,

SOULSPECTION
A Collection of Poetry

MICHELLE BOREL

iUniverse

SOULSPECTION
A COLLECTION OF POETRY

iUniverse books may be ordered through booksellers or by contacting:

iUniverse
1663 Liberty Drive
Bloomington, IN 47403
www.iuniverse.com
1-800-Authors (1-800-288-4677)

Because of the dynamic nature of the Internet, any web addresses or
links contained in this book may have changed since publication and
may no longer be valid. The views expressed in this work are solely those
of the author and do not necessarily reflect the views of the publisher,
and the publisher hereby disclaims any responsibility for them.

Any people depicted in stock imagery provided by Thinkstock are
models, and such images are being used for illustrative purposes only.
Certain stock imagery © Thinkstock.

ISBN: 978-1-4917-3558-9 (sc)
ISBN: 978-1-4917-3560-2 (hc)
ISBN: 978-1-4917-3559-6 (e)

Library of Congress Control Number: 2014909475

Print information available on last page.

iUniverse rev. date: 07/28/2016

This book is dedicated to my family
Especially my wonderful children
Elijah Omarie, Cheydaa Emily and Faith Elizabeth
I love you all beyond words
And
Bless you!

Introduction

I believe in life when we laugh, cry, rise, fall and rise again it is in vain, if we do not share our stories with those who come into our life. There is something that we can learn from everyone. I do hope that these pieces I have compiled over these years are able to speak to you positively. My thought is that creativity links us with our Creator. That being the case, don't bury your talents, as the best way to say thank you for the gifts you have received is to use them.

This book is not only a way of sharing with you, but also it is my way of utilizing the talents I have been blessed with and saying – Thank you!

Not everything I write about I have experienced firsthand. There are some stories that either friends or family have shared with me or I may have observed and chose to write about it, as it may give someone comfort, healing, hope or understanding.

I didn't want to focus on one topic for this book, because I believe poetry is a form of expression and I had a lot to let out. Together with that, I wanted it to be a book for all occasions and various emotions. A book that you can grow with, move with, learn with and cry with; Maybe even enjoy with someone else at your side.

I am truly grateful for the time you will be taking to read this!

Contents

Me

I Am

I'm not a raffle so with me there are no chances.
I'm a woman, no longer a girl given to glances.
My mind is focused, it no longer dances
and I clearly articulate what my stance is.

I'm not a taxi so with me there are no rides.
I'm a woman, no longer a girl wanting to be one of the brides.
My decisions I make when my feeling subsides
and my beauty can be seen even though my face hides.

I'm not a toy so with me there are no games.
I'm a woman, no longer a girl crying of pains.
My stare can penetrate deeper than burning flames
and I'm not given to calling names.

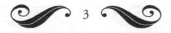

I'm not a phone so with me there's no holding on.
I'm a woman, not a girl chasing after what is gone.
My heart is like a phoenix it can be reborn
And I know there is power in letting go and moving on . . .

The Sun

Under the sun is my home
I hope to stay
But I'm sure adventure would call
some hot day.

I would leave home
I love so dear,
But I would always return
Back here.

For I would miss the penetration
of sun on my back
the filtration of breeze
that other places lack.

In other places the weather
Keeps hearts cold,
but under the sun they thaw out
your spirit never grows old.

Under the sun is my family—
Sister, mother
and not to forget my darling honey,
Aunts and brother,
All of we is one family.
So, big up to the sun
and this sweet country.

Trinidad & Tobago

I come from the land
of steel pan and calypso.
Our national birds are:
The Scarlet Ibis and Cocorico.

Our main income
is not having tourists,
but if you are travelling—
Put us on your list!

Visit the Devil's Wood yard
to witness mud volcanoes
Or lime with friends on Brian Lara Promenade;
Named after a national hero.

Can't forget our Pitch Lake—
It's in Deep South, La Brea.
About Douen and Papa Bois folklore
Hear what villagers have to say.

When on Maracas Beach
Bake n' Shark is a staple.
Try some hot pepper called 'Mother-in-Law,'
if you think your taste buds able.

Drive down Matelot
Keshon Walcott is from there,
and if the breeze is forceful
you'll smell spices in the air.

Buccoo Reef in Tobago
is a must-see attraction.
Also, do an estate tour,
but, secure a reservation.

Enjoy our 'heritage food':
Cow, pig, chicken or conch souse.
Crab n' dumpling, callaloo will leave you
Looking like a house.

Store Bay is another popular spot!
T & T has a lot for you to treasure
But, our nation's greatest gem—The PEOPLE
Who are warm and friendly beyond measure.

Jewel

Many have tried
and many have failed
only to one
Will I be unveiled.

A jewel,
Is what I am.
I cannot be held
by every man.

For this jewel
take off the outer crust,
over come
that spirit of lust.

Dig and dig,
See what you find.
Don't let the exterior
make you blind.

Great rewards
await you on the other side.
The value
is on the inside.

With this jewel
you will be pleased
for you did not obtain it
with ease.

Me vs You

There is a boy that I love so,
but my family thinks he is faux.
I once allowed their views to control me,
but then of what value is the two-letter word "me?"

Throughout my life, I allowed myself to be molded.
Like my mother's laundry, I was tucked and folded.
I was loved for who I was not
and the person inside, one forgot.

But when the tables turned around,
Instead of smiles, I got frowns.
I won the battle, as you can see,
because now, I am responsible for who I be.

Fool No More

Was once a fool in love,
But I am a fool no more.
Time has finally developed
my inner core.

No longer do I need to be loved
nor do I have to feel it
for within me . . .
Within my being I possess it!

Still with the one
To whom I was madly in love with,
But realized that love didn't mean
I was a carpet.

I got up
and I stood tall
and told myself
I can do it all.

With or without
Family and friends
I have to run the race of life
and conquer it in the end.

Let Me Be

You say that life
is not so cut and dry.
Yet, on your bed
you sit and lie,
expecting all you want
to fall from the sky.
I am an extreme—
Am I?

My goals I write
with paper and pen.
Then, I get up
and fight till the end,
knowing I can get nothing
if I sit on my rear end.
Only on God
Will I depend.

Who are you
to judge me?
When you have not
my eyes to see . . .
Just allow me to be me
and there'll be productivity.
For I shall never become
one of passivity.

Changing For Whom?

I was afraid of who I was then
So I changed my life
And started all over again
Trying to be
Who or what they wanted me
Trying to fit in.

I am afraid of who I am now
So I want to go back
But I just don't know how
I don't want to be
Who or what they want me
I want to fit into what makes me, me.

Free

In the name of the Father, Son and Holy Spirit, One God
They baptized me.
I went in the water a slave
and came out FREE!

No longer am I in bondage.
I have a new name. It is Fekerte Selassie
and I represent the Most High,
I am love of the Trinity.

I need not kill, steal or lie
to survive anymore.
I depend not on man!
So, I do not as before.

I Believe!

I believe in one Triune God
Jesus Christ is My Lord and Savior
Quickly I repent
if contrary is my behavior.

I keep my eyes up and up,
because I am looking for only what is heaven sent.
Only for MY GOD
Will I allow my knees to be bent . . .

What I always keep in my heart is that
all things work for the greater good for those who love
the Lord!
So, thankfully I give praises . . .
Heavenly Father, YOU do I applaud!

Royalty

I'm human; I gave into a feeling
that's considered natural.
I'm not going to give details
and get all factual.

I've got to forget about nature
and nurture within something Divine.
Can't walk into the trap
another time.

At this time, don't think
I could even be his friend
for just by his touch
to the floor does my body want to descend.

Second fiddle
never will I allow myself to be
for I stand tall
as empress 'Fekerte Selassie.'

Love of the Trinity
has been implanted within my core
Knowing the royalty I am
I will not cheapen myself by acting as a whore.

Passions and lusts of the flesh
will not suffice.
True satisfaction is felt
when heart and mind also entice.

The pain within
Will I carry.
For gain will I
the victory.—

Knowing that I discovered the lie
from man's tongue,
'At this time,
I don't have anyone.'

Knowing that I maintained
Love and respect
for a lady
I have never even met.

Knowing that before I was completely weakened
I regained control
and didn't allow that feeling
to become whole.

Knowing that if destiny sanctions it
so shall it be.
But be will it,
with me as ROYALTY!

Blinded By the Look

What are my imperfections? I am as pretty as can be.
Yet, many only see ugliness in me.

I do not smell like flowers, I do not look like pearls,
I do not feel like satin and I laugh not like other girls.

There are marks all over my long oval face,
I have sad puffy eyes and have not a petite waist.

However, I am pretty, as pretty as can be.
My heart, as pure as gold, is an essential part of me.

Had I not a good heart, how would I survive?
Everyone knows it is the heart that keeps you alive.

Many do not realize my skin is just a foil.
Unwrap the skin, dig deep down, you'll find I am as rich
as oil.

Oh, ain't I pretty as pretty as can be!
Sorry for those who have not eyes to see . . .

Family

Never Any Other

With joy I think of my mother
for she made a choice others neglect.
I thank her for her eyes
for not one day have they shown a sign of regret.

When I hurt, when I stumble, when I cry . . .
I know she feels it more than I.
and it's my troubles that keep her up
Though morning is nigh.

I can fly, yet still I know
her wings will receive me.
When needed I can return to the nest
and she will still feed me.

Her feelings she tries to hide,
but her actions show love and affection.
Never rough, never brutal
was her rod of correction.

With all she does
Nothing does she ask for as compensation.
And never has she wanted
any form of gratification.

What she has given
another person cannot.
And, as her child I can easily overlook
her character's dark spots.

Though these words can never be enough
I say thank you to my mother.
Both she and time have shown me
there can never be any other.

My Husband

From very early on he said
That it would be me who he would marry.
I laughed thinking he was playing
And that that would be less than likely.

Yet, down I walked that isle
As his youthful blushing bride.
His wife—A role
I would hold on to with pride.

Many storms came our way
After the last, we thought we couldn't rebuild.
We couldn't! It was God that did!
Us being united was HIS WILL!!!

He loves me so much
That he loves anything and anyone who is of me.
Even when I was blinded,
He still had eyes to see . . .

Many of us are wrong many times,
but not many of us are ever truly sorry.
We all have our flaws,
but not all of us work on correcting them daily!

I knew him even before he was tested
and placed in the fire.
Now that he is gold,
I am the only one that he desires.

Each prayer I prayed was a coal
that aided in who now stands before me—
From boy to man I have seen him grow
And still shower him with prayer daily.

Being a Mother

I hold you in my arms and I feel warmth
I look at your little nose, mouth and eyes . . .
Quietly I promise you and I
That I will ease all your cries . . .

Anyone who has never held you
I think to myself has never held love
Experiencing being a mother solidifies
That there is a God above.

Often do I softly kiss
your little fingers and your toes
and like an angel you smile
when I rub my nose on your nose.

Your eyes are peaceful while you are sleeping
they are bright when you are awake.
Everyone is filled with laughter
by the cooing sounds you make.

10,000 *Pampers Later*

10,000 pampers later
Upon a stage I stared
Looking at this lady who
Was once a child I reared
Thinking it was worth it
Every problem that I bared
And remembering precious memories
That with her I shared . . .

10,000 pampers later
He grew from baby, to boy to man
And as I wobbled down the street
He was there to hold my hand.
Long are the days of cuts and bruises
He puts together business plans . . .
He moved from his room to his own house
And owns businesses, cars and land!

10,000 pampers later
There were no more sleepless nights
But this woman of grandeur and grace
Was the focus in the spotlight
No more time outs for naughty ways
She was committed to doing right
Proudly I would stand
As I witness such a sight . . .

Daughters

Delicate Flowers

All flowers have petals
Nectar is craved by all bees
Scents may differ,
but they are all carried by the breeze.

A flower is a product
of the seed,
but good soil
is another need.

Even if not touched
all petals fall,
but pruning
is most important of all!

Bees will buzz
and flowers have to grow
Remember that you reap
what you sow!

Fence your garden
Be selective with who's picking
Not on every table
Can flowers be sitting . . .

Keep flowers
As delicate as they are meant to be
Flowers are not for all to have,
But just to see . . .

If a flower is deflowered
Then let it be
To one,
Who has pledged solemnly . . .

I Can't Now

I will, I do, I can't . . .
I mean I can,
But I won't.
I want to love you,
but then I don't.
Not that way . . .
But will you,
Please stay?

I want to do things right,
It's not that
I don't want to hold you at night,
But I have to put up this fight.
When I walk down the aisle,
I want my gown and veil to be white.
Understand baby,
please take it light.
I am reserved for my wedding night.

I will, I do, I can't . . .
Not now I can,
and I won't.
I want to love you,
but I can't.
Not now anyway . . .
After we marry,
you may have your way!

There Still?

I've never been
the type to date
as with me
it either is or it ain't.

Only now
I look back and remember
how your eyes addressed me
and undressed me tender.

I thought you touching me
Was accidental at that time,
but realize now
That it was you throwing your line.

I was naive
till I was stupid.
To think what followed next
I thought was cupid!

We laughed, we shared,
and we spoke deeper.
Instantly we clicked
or is it that the drink was a creeper?

I was off to bed
but you insisted I stay.
I should not have listened!
I should have gone my way . . .

You shared secrets
and I shared mine.
Then, what your eyes revealed
was a crime.

Two sets of lips
made four
and your body said
that you wanted more.

I shook my head
and tried to wait.
I questioned
if this would be a mistake.

So, for a night or two
we won the battle with temptation
until one plus one equaled one
in this equation.

Good sense prevailed
I thought we must quit,
But you insisted you knew what you wanted
and that I was it!

Yet time showed
that my quieter feeling inside was right.
Somehow our math was wrong
as one plus one made three that night.

The lesson in this
is that time will reveal
and another thing with time
is that it does heal!

I grew learning
that a lady is a flower,
but on my own I learnt
we women have power!

One may want now,
but it is best if you wait until—
Until more time passes
and whether or not they are there still!

Male Fertility

There's a difference between
A father and a daddy
It takes more
Than male fertility

Daddy is the one—
Who takes care of the baby
Treating the mama
Always like a lady . . .
His actions are direct—
Never shady!
No need to wonder
Where he's been lately
Because he is proud
To be someone's daddy,
Even if it is not so
Biologically

There's a difference between
A father and a daddy
It takes more
Than male fertility

A father in his mind thinks
That he was not ready.
Always unstable
Never steady.
No problem in
Him bedding a roni,
But somehow isn't present
To tuck in his baby
Concerning the child –
He stamps MAYBE
Appears just cool
To act irresponsibly

There's a BIG difference between
A father and a daddy
It takes more
Than male fertility

God's Teaching

I cried out to God
Every time I got a blow.
My body felt pain
And my spirit said, 'Jah know, Jah know!'

Tears dropped
And so did my knees to the floor
'Abba, Father, please . . .
No more, no more . . .'

But it was a situation
I put myself in
For without God,
We could never win!

Emotionally too
was I cut
And that hurt me more
than being kicked in the gut.

Signs telling me, 'Beware!
Do not enter here!'
I ignored
and still went there.

The greatest sign
Was a feeling inside
that whispered,
'Here love does not reside . . .'

There was no peace,
No tranquility
and every mishap
we blamed the enemy.

But I knew then
and know even now
That God will make good
of this mess somehow.

I understand more
by the practical part of God's teaching
what is for you is for you
and within feels calm and soothing.

Love

What Attracts One to Thee?

I used to believe that one's eyes were the window to one's soul.
Gazing into another's eyes it is easy for one to get lost in another world.
A world of mystery, a world of illusion, a world not of our own—
'What if I couldn't see? What if God didn't give the gift of sight to me?'
I thanked God for this gift and changed my analogy.
For if one can't see, then, there must be some other force that compels one to thee.

I then believed that one's voice was captured by another's ears—
Luring one on by words carefully placed, creating a rhythmic tune for a dance of seduction to take place.
A song of passion, a song of deception, a song which irregulates the heart's pace.
But, with tape on my mouth and cotton in my ears, I wondered, 'What if I couldn't speak nor hear? What if someone couldn't hear the words I had to spare?'
I thanked God for these blessings and changed my analogy—
For if one couldn't hear nor speak, or lacked just one of these then it would not make any sense to capture love with any of these.

I later believed that one's sense of smell attracted one to thee.
Hell! The birds and bees do it, so why can't we?
A woman who smells like roses could send pulsations to a man's brain.
A scent of tantalization, a scent of elevation, a scent that eases pain.

But with tubes in my nose and unable to smell, I reflected,
'What if I could never smell again? What if I was unable
to smell perfume or blueberry pie?'
I thanked God for being able to smell and changed my
analogy—
For if one couldn't smell, then, this is not what draws one
to thee!

Then, I believed that it was all in one's body movement
and a sensualistic touch.
The way one walks, moving each limb, one can be
hypnotized and feeling the heat of a foreign body doesn't
seem like a sin.
A move of sensual-ism, a move of temptation, a move that
could make one's head spin.
But, if I had not legs, I wondered,
'What would the case be? What if I were crippled or
another unable to see?'
For if one could not see this movement, then, of what value
would it be?

So, allow me to state that an attraction is a trivial thing
dealing with sight, taste, touch and sound, which in
determining love means nothing.
For a soul needs none of these things as it communicates
in a way that I cannot explain.
But, it tickles the heart and makes it smile and not like
those outer assets, which pleases one only for a little while.

This Heart

Here is my heart!
You can take it with you . . .
If there is harm,
it will shelter you.

If doors close before you,
its love is the key to unlock them.
If there is chaos,
it will keep you from mayhem.

Should disaster strike
it is there at your defense.
Should your sins feel heavy
this heart won't give you sentence.

When there is winter
this heart can be a jacket.
All wrongs buried
with the hatchet.

This heart is yours
so don't leave it.
It is here when you want,
But more importantly when you need it

Without

Book without pages,
Pages without words,
Words without meaning,
Meaning without you,
you without me . . .

Those are just things that cannot be!

Make Love to Me

Make love to me
like never before
Let it be with love
That you open a door.

Connection of two souls
Exist not only in bed.
It's in everything that's done,
everything that's said.

Show me your fire
with willing eyes
and beyond the charms of our bodies
will we tantalize.

As I prepare a meal,
the oo's and ah's will start,
Because each addition, each stir
Will come from the depths of my heart.

Freely lend
a helping hand
and the other need not look
for it in a distant land.

Make love to me I say
Like never before
Beyond the bedroom
Give me more!

Misleading

People often mistake
Infatuation for love.
Thinking they really care,
A bond is sealed from above.

Then, of what essence
would marriage be,
if we all make this mistake
so easily?

I'm sad to say,
(Hell no! I'm not!)
But I think abuse
is just plain mutt.

This will happen
if couples try to think for each other
as it takes one to be smart
and a society can be ignorant together.

So, I'm on my knees praying
'God, Father hear my plea!
Guide me on a righteous path
and help me find the one you put on this earth FOR ME!'

My head is bowed down, I'm crying
But I'll wipe those tears,
Because Lord I have faith in You
And I'll wait even if it takes me years.

Love Does That

I felt the chill of the night
without you by my side
I can boldly say 'I miss you'
without any sense of pride . . .

Love does that!
Love has a way of weakening our defense
Love somehow erases all common sense.

I felt the brunt of work,
because I didn't hear your voice today
without thinking twice
I would tell you 'to stay'

Love does that!
Love has a way of weakening our defense
Love somehow erases all common sense.

I felt the weight of the traffic
it was heavy without you in the other seat
Regardless of distance or time
I would demand 'Let's Meet!'

Love does that!
Love has a way of weakening our defense
Love somehow erases all common sense.

At the end of the day
without you home I felt stressed
had you been there
I would have asked 'Why aren't you undressed?'

Love does that!
Love has a way of weakening our defense
Love somehow erases all common sense.

Love Love Love
Love has a million demands
But give to it and overflowing will be your hands

Love does that!
Love has a way of weakening our defense
Love somehow erases all common sense.

Kiss Me Again

So long I did not taste your kiss.
Many a night I sat to reminisce.

Then when you finally kissed me again,
I held on to that feeling, because I didn't want it to end.

I hold my face and remember
that our previous kiss was sweet and tender.

I Wonder How It Feels
to Be Loved – By Me!

I packed my bags, and
Said farewell to my world—
To love, honor and obey
the one to whom I was sold.

But who sold me?
Did I sell myself?
It's a train, a plane,
a puppet. No, an elf!

Man's little helper.
That's what I am!
SO, is this
God's master plan?

Go ahead! Pull a string
And I come to life.
Presto change-o. Ta-da!
A wife!

I wave my wand
and you've got a clean home,
three kids, super
and a throne.

The fairy that changed Pinocchio,
Sprinkled some dust on me.
Now! I can feel, hear, talk,
Think, touch and see!

I can feel my tears;
I can hear your lies.
When I talk,
I see you look surprised.

I can feel your touch.—
It drains me. I am empty.
I wonder how it feels
to be loved—by me.

I wonder how it feels
to be loved—by me.

I wonder how it feels,
to be loved—by me . . .

Some Nights, Some Days . . .

Some nights the moon lies
in the sky, without the stars.
Some nights Venus
Can do without Mars . . .

Some days the sun shines
While the rain falls.
Some days we don't answer
when one calls . . .

Some nights it's hot
and we don't need a sheet.
Some nights, it's ok
if we do not meet.

Some days we don't
Wake hearing birds singing.
Some days it's ok
if one isn't next to us yawning.

Some nights the moon
is bright and full.
Some nights one's body
has gravity pull.

Some days the sun
Shines brighter than the others.
Some days one's hand
cannot do without another's.

Some nights the rain
Descends gently.
Some nights one
wants some sensitivity.

Some days you see
a rainbow in the sky.
Some days one
doesn't want to say good-bye . . .

No Talk of Tomorrow

Don't sing to me of tomorrow
Like the birds let's sing today . . .

Let's rejoice in the morning
and listen to what the trees have to say!

Though dark clouds may be around,
like the sun let's still shine!

I can't say what is to come,
but at least for now you are mine!

May our bodies dance to the same beat—
One two three, one two three, one two three four

May our souls sing the same song,
'Every moment I love you more and more!'
Our spirits embrace
so miles now wither . . .

From a distance if there is no you tomorrow
You still hear me call, 'Come hither . . .'

Let us not even think of tomorrow
we have been blessed with today.

Hold me tightly; kiss me sweetly
as with me you have your way . . .

Satisfaction

Satisfaction goes deeper than between my thighs
You can get that from anyone who bats their eyes
Within the depths of my soul satisfaction lies
It is not found in moaning and late night cries . . .

Satisfaction lasts longer than a rhythmic gasp
You can get that whether you're alone or hands in clasp
Beneath my flesh does satisfaction bask
It is not heard in the yes of what at night you ask.

Satisfaction is stronger than when you thrust
You can get that from anyone after whom you lust
Rooted in me is satisfaction's bust
It is not as easily blown away as dust!

Love of My Youth

Do you remember us as teens?
Constantly we yearned for each other
and not for long
could one do without the other!

It all started on a couch
In the living room of my mother
Had she known never again
Your name would I be allowed to utter . . .

Every lonely space
Was christened by our youth
Had my daddy known
He would have used his gun to shoot!

To unlock our lips
there was no key
and now we are tied in marriage
celebrating another year of you and me.

Keep Hope! Keep Loving!

Here's a toast to all of those
Who have been in love or are still loving
Or better yet those who have lost their love
But have not lost their hoping . . .

Those who know what it is to miss a touch
That they loved so much
And still have hope
To again have such!

Those who have lost words exchanged
That fit so tightly like a finished puzzle
By not just their lover, but their friend
For whom they didn't need a muzzle.

How about those who lost the beauty
They saw in a smile,
Yet can still hold on to hope longer,
As they convince themselves, 'It will only be a while . . .'

Let's not forget those who thought
They'll be in each other's arms till time's end.
I toast to you for your love has hope
As its lifelong friend.

Cheers! Cheers! Cheers to life
Which is not life without love . . .
Cheers to those who have been blessed with a second
chance
For your hope has been crowned from above . . .

Love is an Action

Oh how you love me
And I love you too
You will always be my first
Now you're my last too
I always questioned
If your love was true
But now I am convinced
Because of what you continue to do

Others took advantage
Of a tender heart
You were there for me
Even when we were apart
Though we were separated
You gave us a fresh start
And of our family
Made her a part.

I could cry and talk to you
about anything
you are my best friend, my husband
the rightful king.
In our youth
we had our wedding
yet continue to rise
despite all momentary suffering.

With this renewed and solid love
I appreciate that you let me be
and I thank God
and bless you daily.
We have been pruned
and have grown into a solid tree
our story proving
that we were meant to be!

Heartbreak

The Moon Cries

The moon—The world's crystal ball
In her bed of dark velvet sheets wept that night
Knowing that never again your smile, eyes—YOU
Would bless my earthly sight!

We unknowingly danced
in her long never ending tears
Unaware that we would be separated
by life not days, months or years . . .

Her sobbing kept us up
and we silenced it by our touching
our lips exchanged gifts
when no one was watching!

We sheltered in each other's arms
and our hearts we offered as warmth
the generations within your loins fed me
as sensually I seemed gaunt.

We knew not the reason behind her tears
yet with her that night we cried
and ours sounded like music
as in a room we performed side by side.

The moon knows all secrets
yet tells no tales!
That night she saw our fortune
and evidence of her sorrow filled pails.

Now we understand her grief
you're left to hold one hand and me the other.
Or is it that she stays up late at night to comfort us
as we no longer have each other?

If I Treated You Like Poetry

If I treated you like poetry,
I would watch my every word
and tell you of my untold stories
that no one else has ever heard.

If I treated you like poetry,
not a single emotion would I hide
and I would take you with me
everywhere and tell everyone with pride.

If I treated you like poetry,
I would just let everything flow
and share with you all I possess
and all that I have come to know.

If I treated you like poetry,
each moment would last forever
and maybe now, in looking back,
maybe that's why we aren't together

I Wait For You . . .

I wait for you . . .
I wait for your presence
To grace me
Under the blue moon-
Moon of magic, moon of hope—
Hoping that our love will prosper!

Fear does not grip me
As I await your shadow to appear—
First signal that you have come . . .
Come for me under the blue moon

Fear does not entertain
In the cold darkness
That accompanies our blue moon . . .

Fear does not survive
The safety of me longing
For your love to return . . .

I wait! I wait! I wait for you . . . I wait for you to merge
Out of the gloom my life is
Without you . . .

Under the rarity of the blue moon
Even if it is just once!
Just once, under a blue moon . . .

I wait for you . . . . For you . . . For you and your love . . .

He Was on His Knees

He stares at her cold lifeless body;
not believing she's dead
while warm and spirit filled memories
now fill his head.

He wishes what was put to rest
Was his hurt and regret.
Yet awake are dear times gone by
and now, all he has is a pet.

He cries a cry
from the depths of his soul
yet shallow were his youthful days
which haunt him now that he's old.

She was the one that got away
because he wanted his heart's every desire.
Yet petals fall from all flowers
and it was only her scent that set him afire.

She would speak of heaven,
but he was bound to this earth—
He was guided by greed and lust
forgetting that to dust we all return.

She had a life flooded with joy,
which he saw as he looked around the room.
His was a grave of buried sorrow—
One of them being that his lost love was gone too soon.

He at many times picked up the phone,
but the number of unsaid words were weights on the
receiver.
After all these years he still thought of her
And now, would never have a chance to tell her . . .

He wanted to hold on to her carcass,
But many years ago she let him go;
even though locked inside her
Were feelings no one would ever know!

He thought his tale was more tragic
than that of Romeo and Juliet,
because not only was this love not allowed to be,
but also in mortality her he would never get.

She moved on with her life.
It was life, and she lived it!
She tied herself to another man
and with their kids did the man sit.

She brightly smiled
in a picture at the top of her casket,
while sitting in the back with long silent tears
He placed money in the collection basket.

She would live forever
in his memories
and praying for her soul's transition
was the first time in years he was on his knees.

The Letter

I expressed feelings that I was first willing to hide.
However, I brought out all I have inside.
Then, came your response and something died.

In return for my passion I got practicality.
This was not the same person who once said that they
love me.
It was my truth that unmasked your prior hypocrisy.
A giant would have had the bravado to speak freely!

Respond I won't because I have value.
The only question mark is next to you.
Character is determined by what you did or didn't do,
Not by words that you give someone to chew.

Hurt

Sixteen

It was meant to be the party of my life
and my life did it change.
The word fun
was somehow rearranged.

Let me take you back
back to that butterfly feeling
I had my dress—it was backless
and my dad nearly hit the ceiling.

Mom though said that it was ok
Ok for me to dress that way
I was never the type of girl
To go astray . . .

My sister combed my hair—
Hair was long and flowing on my back.
At sixteen I was shy
And didn't know how to act.

I heard the door bell and started screaming
Screaming with excitement
As this memory in time
I wanted to cement.

Glitter dust was in my eyes
Eyes that were windows to my anticipation.
To my date
my parents got an introduction.

After pictures,
Pictures of my innocent intents,
did we leave to frolic
and on the night make our dent.

Funny though the party I don't remember much
Much of what happened faded
After the incident
All was jaded . . .

Ten years later
Later and it is still playing in my head
The nasty feeling inside
Makes me wish I was dead.

He touched me where
Where my mother said no one must dare
He ripped my clothes
And what he did next my body couldn't bear.

I held my head as I screamed,
'No! Don't do it! No! No! Nooooooooo . . .'
After he threatened my life
And said what happened there no one must know!

Inside I have been crying
Crying because I never was the same
And what's worse is that no one ever asked
Why my eyes carry now so much pain . . .

Within Her

36-25-46
Did she measure
As she walked down the street
Eyes tasted her look with pleasure
Some even remarked,
'Wow! What a figure!'
But they knew not
What was within her

The clicking of her stilettos
Sounded to passersby like a rhythm
Instantly
Guys seemed smitten
They tried to persuade
Her kitty kit kitten
But they had no idea
What she had on a paper written

When she spoke
It sounded more like singing
For her
Smiles were beaming
Mid way
Some felt a tingling
But they were unaware
What this lady was thinking.

Her face was like the sky
As you could stare at it for hours
You would think her intense blue eyes
Had hidden powers
Like prey, her
They were ready to devour
But no one knew why
Her doctor's visit made her sour . . .

Voice of Innocence

Daddy please daddy please
Were my cries
Daddy please please please
Don't go between my thighs
Daddy no daddy no
Look at the innocence in my eyes
Daddy daddy daddy
I can't tell mummy lies . . .

Mummy why why why
Did daddy do this to me
Why mummy why
Do you pretend not to see
Mummy mummy mummy
Because of you I be
Mummy mummy mummy
Please hear my plea

Bother sister help me
Help me if you can
Brother sister please
We call him daddy but know not that man
Brother sister please please please
Reach out your hand
Brother sister why why why
Why you act like you give not a damne

Granny hear me granny please
My body did he use
Granny granny listen
That's how I got this bruise
Granny granny granny
Question daddy about my muddy shoes
Granny please please please
This I didn't choose

Listen teacher! Listen stranger! Listen friend
On you right now does my life depend!!!

Strength

Forgiveness

Forgiveness is never
about you and the perpetrator,
but you
And Your Creator.

Regardless of what,
choose to always be a lover
as you can't be blessed
as a hater . . .

Protection

I worship You Lord
In my heart day and night
Thank You for removing
My sins and transgressions from Your sight
All my battles
I give to You to fight
Ensure that in Your eyes
I am upright
Don't let me fall Lord
Hold me tight!
Destroy the wicked ways
of my enemies with all Your might!

The Sun Will Rise

I close my eyes and look within—
Saddened by the horror of my sin.

Would I ever return to Paradise?
I lost it, with the role of a dice.

I cry, I fast, I beg to be forgiven.
Yet still, this land is 'Forbidden'—I forsaken.

I opened a box and out came turmoil,
I must now struggle and toil.

Ten thousand sorries cannot right my wrong.
Over, over, over and over, I sing my song.

Wait! I can see a prolific light.
Soon, very soon, it will null the night.

Start Anew

Every day you rise,
you rise a new man;
and everything you are
Is in Your father's hands.

So every day,
Give Him thanks and praise.
Through His grace
you'll have lengthier days.

All you are
is all the almighty makes you.
So, ensure that
you pay Him His due.

He is the Merciful Master
who has freed us our sins.
Turn to Him,
because your daily battles He must win!

Happy New Day!

The cling cling sound of glasses
the popping sound of a bottle of champagne
Smiles, kisses and laughter
as everyone shouts the same refrain

Time is flattered by the attention
yet quickly suffers the reality of fame.
For a minute they knew her,
but now can't remember her name.

Why only for this moment was she relevant
When throughout she tic tic tocs your day?
For life she goes with you,
yet sometimes you ignore and go your way.

Look at her and revere her
not only as you say 'Happy New Year'
But every morning celebrate with your loved ones
Because your eyes are open—you are here!

Watering Strength

There's nothing I can do
that can make you happy.
If you were to feel joy
it would just be.

Washing wears, hot meals,
clean sheets can't change a man,
only the heart and will
of an individual can.

To think I came back
to improve in areas where I lacked,
Hoping it would change
A tongue and pants that were slack.

Nothing I can do—
For to me you do not belong
and it's my fault
that I cry the same song.

I have allowed myself
to be cast into prison
Not speaking out
was my decision.

Same way I can't
make you happy,
Is the same way
I can't make you hit me.

Provoked you say
you are,
yet my heart and body
each carry a scar.

My heart is hurting
from cruel words and rejection.
My body is paining
from anger's infliction.

Tears I've cried
won't be wasted
so plentiful were they
that the earth has tasted.

May my tears of sorrow
Water seeds of strength
that grow tall enough to shelter me
from life's torments.

Life

Personalities

Of personalities, there are many!
They can be similar, but never the same,
And here's something to consider,
Even though firstly you think it profane;

Fierce dogs are usually at the front
Of a house where valuables may lie . . .
So, before you judge another
Truly give them an honest try.

I ask you please to consider
That a clam in it may hold a pearl
And when dealing with personalities
Remember, it takes all kinds to make up the world.

We Shine

We shine, but are shaded
By intricate chandelier.
Delicate string
Connecting crystals . . .
Peeping light displays
Beauty—not intent
As a poisonous flower
As a seducer
As dirt covering treasure

Man and Beast

Could demon and angel co-exist?

Does the wheat not grow with the tares?

Who would ever believe under a bed of roses was the home of all my fears?

Man and monster share the same form
gravitating from an iceberg cold to a sea breeze warm.
Yet, in all of us, is that not at times the norm?

North is as close to south, as east is as far from west
And is it not that the one you hate at times becomes your love interest?
Doesn't the mother who hatched the egg
later push the bird from the nest?

Could the sun and rain share the sky?

Does not life and death lie in a trigger?

Who would ever believe that sweet grapes in time can taste bitter?

Deeds Are Round
& Actions Revisit

The world is round
and so too are our deeds.
A person is not paper
cut him, he bleeds.

Now you are crying,
but dry your eyes.
Instead remember
when you told hurtful lies.

The waves of the ocean
Return to the sea.
Think of how
you want your life to be.

What you would like for you
give to others.
Remember you are the keep
of your brothers.

Every night the moon
revisits the sky.
With what we do
there is no goodbye.

'Welcome back' past actions
can say to you.
So, careful now
what and to whom you do . . .

Mother Earth

Oh, Mother Earth!
I can feel your hurt,
as they walk on you like dirt.
Oh, Mother Earth!
I can feel your hurt.

They slice you, they dice you
and then, they price you.
How they misuse you, abuse you.
Mother earth, this is an issue.

Unable to stand, you quake and fall . . .
and your wicked seeds say, 'She's old, that's natur-all.'
That's not their problem, so they can laugh at it all
and carry on with their bauble.

On you that raised them, they turn their backs.
As a result of what they stole, you lack!
But seventy-seven times seven shall their deeds multiply.
They will be sorry and regretful the day you die.

Oh, Mother Earth! Mother Earth!

Guests

Usually as a guest
you are on good behavior.

You try to hide the idiosyncrasies
that are of a faulty nature.

We are from this world, but are not of it
we won't live forever.

Here we are only guests
we must return home to Our Maker.

So, I wonder why as guests
we show ill character.

Why do we lie, cheat, steal, kill
And hurt each other?

What about the earth
we all ill treat her?

Some drive their cars
and throw out paper!

Now take note
that if we continue to litter,

we will destroy the beauty
for other guests to enjoy in the future.

We Are One

We are representative
Of where we were born
And also, of who
We were born from
So, if I say I am African
Isn't that wisdom?
Yet, following that same concept
Is also troublesome
As our ancestors are many –
English, Chinese, Syrian and Indian
In this day and age,
Is anyone truly Caucasian?
Who really knows
All that happened on the plantation?
So why fuel
Any racial frustration
Let's focus on us all being
Of and from the same nation
And too, don't we all profit
From the acts of globalization
Yet, somehow race
Is still a topic of conversation?
By now you would think
The concept of oneness had more penetration
However, there are minds in which
That thought had no fertilization
And they hyphenate who they are
And where they come from,
But let's now band together
And think as one
End result being
That it doesn't matter what region.

Foreigners We Are

We are all worlds
within this world that we share
Another's life
we might be unable to bare.

Foreigners are we
to each other!
Can't we appreciate
the beauty of another?

Knowing we are visitors
we are never meant to stay.
Therefore, forgive quickly
and make the most of everyday!

What's My Inheritance?

A scramble for a dollar
That still can't pay rent
A fight for one's earnings
Which they saved cent by cent
Useless to them now
As in heaven it can't be spent
The only fee accepted
Is a heart that's willing to repent.

Those left behind
The shares they aren't sharing
They testify that of every penny
They are deserving
Money once received

There's no preserving
Like a whore after its duty
There's no returning

Accounts drained
Nothing more is flowing
Memories are all that's left –
Was this someone worth knowing?
Within you
Are seeds of love still growing?
In the end,
That's all we may be holding!

May your estate
Be one that a court can't divide
Assets truly are
What you have inside –
Time, thoughts, teachings
Are what truly gives us pride
Leave a map of lasting treasure
That through life can be a guide.

L.I.P. = Live In Peace

My new home's roof was the earth
and so too was its foundation
It was filled with peace
No talk of work or frustration.

Its welcome mat was of stone
But not all could enter
There was a special message
It had to render:

L.I.P.
Live In Peace don't wait till you are resting
This ephemeral life is check 1 check 1-2-3
Only a testing . . .

Tears of loved ones
Washed my sins away
But my message is to those
Who have been blessed with another day.

My home was lighted
by the brightness of flowers
which the moon shined on
in the midnight hour.

My staircase
was six feet under
those at the top
Left to ponder

but my message
I let it R.I.P.
Reminding all
each day to L.I.P.

Reaching the Golden Light

It wasn't like the TV shows
there was no waiting room.
It was dependent on the time of the Master
So, there was no 'Gone Too Soon!'

It started with a dark tunnel
that held at the end a golden light,
But forces came to battle
To reach it would be a fight.

Futile are our efforts
we can't do it on our own.
Remember to call on Jesus
He won't leave you alone!

The weights of hell can't pull you down
With Jesus holding your hand—
He is King of kings, Lord of lords
they must obey His command.

The raging darkness crept away
there was now nothing but light
Choirs of angels lifted their voices
singing of our good Lord's power and might.

Fulfilled was every promise
a wall of jasper and a city of pure gold,
who was sick and wounded no longer were
As they were made whole.

Every kind of precious stone
at the walls foundation were before your eyes.
Because of the light of God's glory
Sun and moon aren't needed by the skies . . .

Holy, holy, holy is Our Lord Our God
With peace and joy is sung night and day
To be a part of this beauty eternally
With you let Jesus have His way . . .

AWAKENED

We awake to our reality
In our eternal slumber
The lullabies of hymns sung
As we are treated as lumber
Shaded are memories
While we were dreaming
We are awakened
To life's true meaning

Intuition comes to fruition
And performs its duty
Oh what a sight!
Oh what ardent beauty!
We rise like the sun
In its morning glory
The forever sleep
Solves life's mystery

Shedding Pain

The hurt boiled inside
and like a thief crept silently into his bones
the pain gripped him tightly
Horrific were the moans . . .

Childhood memories began to play
so too did his regret, mistakes and longings
Tears ran a marathon down his face
as his heart felt a throbbing.

His body no longer felt a pain
as it was that severe and intense.
Past wrongs came knocking,
but there would be no recompense.

Doors not of this world he ignored,
Yet death did not wait for him to say, 'Come in . . .'
One is left to wonder
in his heart did he repent from sin?

Looking like it was a mere slumber
His body did they shake,
But his eyes visited the back of his head
Never did he wake!

So rise like the morning sun my brother
like a caterpillar become now a butterfly . . .
Let your spirit kiss the cheeks of those who love you
Hush now every cry!

Agony is now behind you
look back no more!
Just smile as before you
is heaven's open door . . .

Black Gold! Black Pride!

Black queen, brown sugar, brown skin
Rembunction, D'Angelo, India Arie all knew what they
were talkin'!
Products of tortured slaves—mixed races expose your
blackness within!
White man tried to infiltrate the kingdom, but strong is
the menelin.

Curly hair, kinky hair, hair like wool—
Wear it out, wear it proud . . . it's nice and full.
Don't let them deceive you, your hair doesn't need that
chemical pull.
Lion and lioness are we in this concrete jungle!

Empress diet pills not for we!
Be proud of hips that represent fertility,
A waist that shows your femininity
And breasts that say, 'You can find comfort in me!'

Implants they are using to try to get our luscious lips.
Don't look for them to give us pips.
Instead on things like diet and exercise they want to give us tips.
As always they try to rule, but away with the whips!

Angie Stone, let's hear it for our black brothers once again!
For only a strong black Mandingo warrior could've endured the middle passage till the end.
With drums, messages did they send.
No matter how much pressure was applied our roots and culture did they defend.

Shades, tones and colors in endless varieties—
Embrace all and spread African unity.
Home will always be Mother Afrika no matter what our nationality.
Let us stand together knowing our identity!

Words of Power

We rated Obama for his, 'Yes we can!'
But, didn't we know that already?
Yes I can do all things
Through Christ Jesus who strengthens me!

We give thanks to those fore fathers
who formed the constitution . . .
But we need to be grateful
For God's Divine instruction!

We remember Dr. Seuss for saying,
'Don't cry because it's over, smile because it happened.'
Yet we must also recall that God's children
He will strengthen!

'So many books, so little time,'
were the words of Frank Zappa,
But in all honesty apart from the Bible and dictionary
not many other books even really matter!

'If you don't stand for something you will fall for anything,'
Is a popular Malcolm X refrain.
So, as Bob Marley croons, 'Get up! Stand up!'
Let's do that, but in Jesus' precious name.

Words

Whatever would we do
without words?
Then, the voice of our soul
will never have been heard.

Yet, funny how though words assist
they are never enough
and that when we are overflowing with emotion
our voice may sound rough!

Then, some of us
Are not always able to articulate
And the rest of us, speak firmly
though inside may shake.

Sometimes to deceive
one may use words to over compensate.
They use it to hide
the invisible web of hate.

Yet, shy of words
May be one who is in love
As such a feeling
May have one as humble as the dove.

Feeling burnt,
Another's words may be like a raging fire
when they really yearn to say,
'I wish it was a reciprocated desire!'

Saddening that pride puts a stopper
on how what we may sincerely like to communicate,
and greed or deceit, on the other hand,
Use words as bait!

Woman

Woman,
I feel your pain
for connected are we
to the same chain.

Woman,
The answer to a hurt nation.
The solution
to a troubled generation.

You,
Stand tall as tall as a tower,
knowing that within you
Lies great power.

Yes,
remember your cries during child birth,
And know for your children
there's no substitution.

Woman,
Mother, sister, daughter, wife . . .
Each share
in the same strife.

Lady,
Keep your heart loving and open.

All your troubles you can handle.
What brought you down
will later be a trophy on your mantle.

Rise up and take your position
for you are woman, you are queen
you have bore seed to a nation.

For Lions Only

For me to call you lion
There are some characteristics you must own.
Firstly, you've got to protect and care for
The seeds that you have sown
I'm not only talking cubs,
But also lioness and territory
As a lion you've got to know
To defend yourself when necessary

For me to call you lion
You have got to be fearless
Stand up against the wrongs
Of which you may be witness
Understanding you are king
Means you don't need to be ruthless
And in every challenge or battle
You put forth your best.

For me to call you lion
Knowing how to hunt is a must
Able to bring down any prey
Be it small, large or with tusk
No timidity when it comes
To rolling around in the dust
And able to perform
Majestically regardless of task

For me to call you lion
Have pride when on a rock you stand alone
And still have no problem with a group
When you roam
Your strength should be seen
Beyond your muscle and bone
Only to greatness
Should you allow yourself to be prone!

Blood of Jesus

Tell yourself that the only blood
That matters, is the blood of Jesus
And we can't just give in
To anything that would please us . . .

Your only true family
is your Heavenly Father up above.
Don't crave attention from anyone.
Give thanks that you have God's love.

Seek not support from others,
know that there's power within.
Speedily go to His throne
and ask forgiveness for your sin.

Friends you may not have,
but you be a friend to all,
and worry not about failure,
Because with the Almighty you will never fall!

Forget about your troubles
As Jesus' blood washes them away
and even if there is sorrow,
Rejoice and be thankful for today!

Appendix

Acknowledgements

First and foremost, I would like to thank my Heavenly Father for life, health, strength and poetry.

I would like to thank my mother for always listening to every poem that I ever wrote without casting any judgment, but instead encouraging me to continue writing. She is a wonderfully passionate individual who has inspired me greatly and I am thankful to be honored enough to call her my mother—Roxanne D. Browne-Phillips, I love you.

My father, Jean Borel I always appreciate our conversations which have helped shape the lady I have grown to be. I am grateful to have you as a father.

To my step father, Kenneth Phillips thank you for being like a father to me and supporting me throughout. For being an awesome and loving grandfather to my three jewels . . . Elijah, Chaydaa and Faith.

To my grandparents (especially my grandmother Elsa Borel), aunts, uncles, cousins, friends and well wishers. I am humbled by your never ending support and encouragement.